the osprey f D0375013 d
to be a sumr
the scotch pine is its homestead
and there it does its best
to be the perfect parent,
a scotch egg in its nest.

Nonsense in Flight

Nonsense in Flight

Drawings and Verses
by
Simon Drew

Five ducks went to church in a box,
(the service was chanted in German);
but the box sprang a leak and submerged
which dampened the end of the sermon.

ANTIQUE COLLECTORS' CLUB

because a bird has no placenta
eggs is how this world they enter

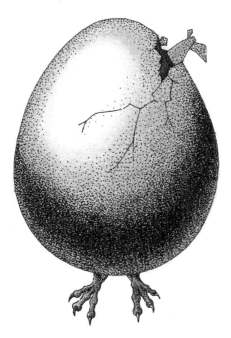

to Caroline,
and to my parents
without whom none of me
would have been possible.

© 1987 Simon Drew
World copyright reserved
First published 1987

ISBN 1-85149-061-2

British Library CIP data
Drew, Simon
    Nonsense in flight.
    I. Title
    828'.91409   PR6054.R4/

All rights reserved. No part of this publication may be reproduced, stored in a retrieval
system or transmitted in any form or by any means electronic, mechanical, photocopying,
recording or otherwise, without the prior permission of the publishers.

Published and printed in England by the Antique Collectors' Club Ltd.,
Woodbridge, Suffolk.

INTRODUCTION

Some people are unaware of some of the extraordinary properties possessed by birds. This group of the animal kingdom is such a strange collection of beasts that they could never have been invented by any human being. Any inventor of merit could never have forgotten arms, for instance; can you imagine designing an animal which is so superb at flying and then forgetting to give it arms and hands for manipulating whatever it has just flown to? Look at the ridiculous way that an egyptian vulture breaks an egg (to eat its contents) by randomly lobbing a stone into the air from its beak.

Could anyone ever have dreamt up the comical absurdities of the puffin, secretary bird, blue stork or penguin?

Obviously evolution has been in progress, resulting in the irregular beings that we know. It is not generally known that the horse evolved from the peacock: this bird used to have the curious habit of landing upside down on its tail feathers. A few birds of the species stayed this way up and passed the characteristic on to their offspring. Illustrated here is the intermediary species which is capable of remaining in either position:

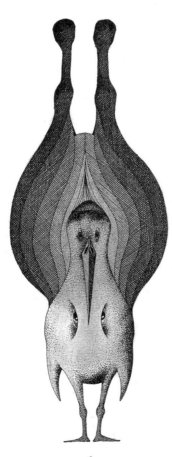

Another notable example of evolution is the development of another bird:

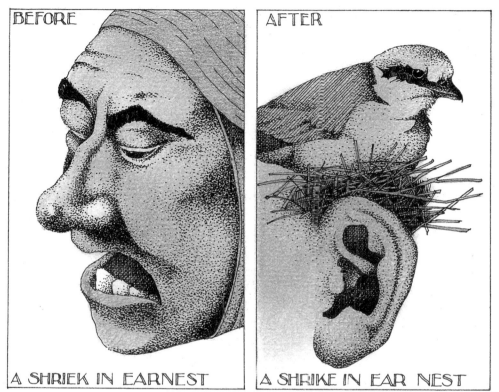

BEFORE

A SHRIEK IN EARNEST

AFTER

A SHRIKE IN EAR NEST

One question remains unanswered: why did birds never evolve wheels? Probably we will never know.

BIRD DROPPING

BREAKFAST, PART ONE

On Tuesday last, without a sound
I'd woken, dressed and gone downstairs
expecting breakfast, but I found
a sight that took me unawares.

The sugar bowl showed signs of feet,
the butter's state you'd call distressed,
the marmalade was far from neat,
and someone had consumed the rest.

BREAKFAST, PART TWO

Today I rose and dressed in haste,
brought in the milk and fetched the post.
I tucked my shirt tails in my waist
and dreamed of scrambled egg on toast.

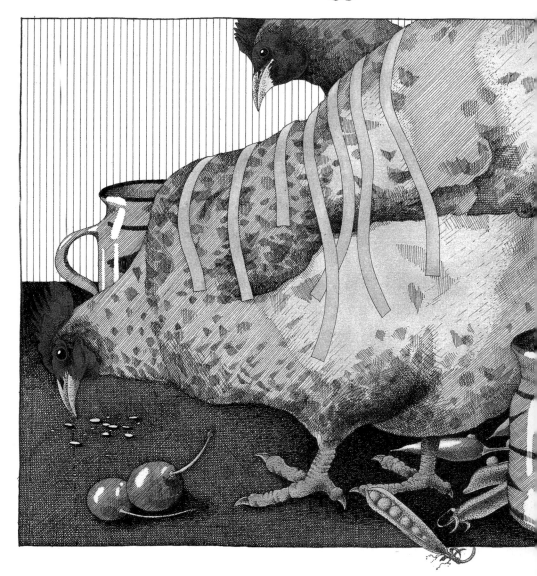

I found there'd been another raid:
(I caught a glimpse of running legs).
The table had been neatly laid
and so had half a dozen eggs.

waders

BLACKBIRD WITH BIN LINERS

WHEN DUCKS HAD APPLES ON THEIR HEADS

In the days when winds blew hard
and Sunday lunch was bread and lard,
people came from miles around
to see a man who was renowned
for training ducks to balance fruit,
although he seemed a callous brute.
Men would gasp with wild delight
to see this acrobatic sight.
Others said with one accord:
"I think this man must be a fraud."
Scrutinized by everyone
and none could guess how it was done.

    o   o   o   o

Maybe it is just as well
they were not seen by William Tell.

THE EVENING DEAR ADA PASSED AWAY

It was after the pastor had said the last rites,
the rooster came in here and turned off the lights;
(and so this is one of those memorable sights
we often recall on the long winter nights).

The cockerel stands beside the sideboard   drew

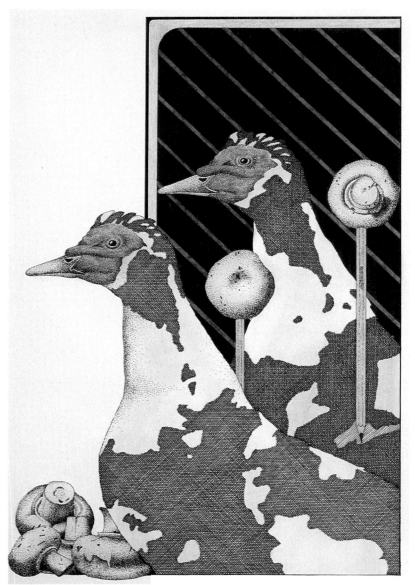

FOUR FUNDAMENTAL FACTS

Did you know that Hardy lived near Dorchester
and pigs in France are learning how to fly
and carthorse is an anagram of orchestra
and geese and mushrooms make a splendid pie?

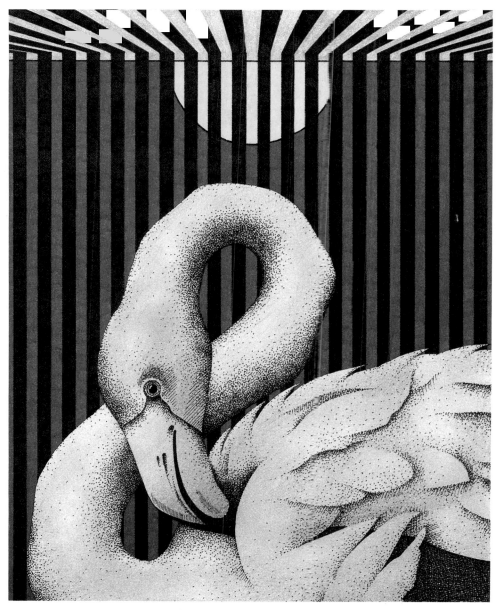

Flamingoes spring naked out of trees
when nobody sees;
and so this act both swift and sordid
has never been recorded.

never eat fish with your fingers: it's rude.
keep your hands clean,
don't play with your food.
(that is the reason the elegant stork
stands on one leg:
it's clutching a fork).

Le déjeuner sur l'herbe avec deux canards

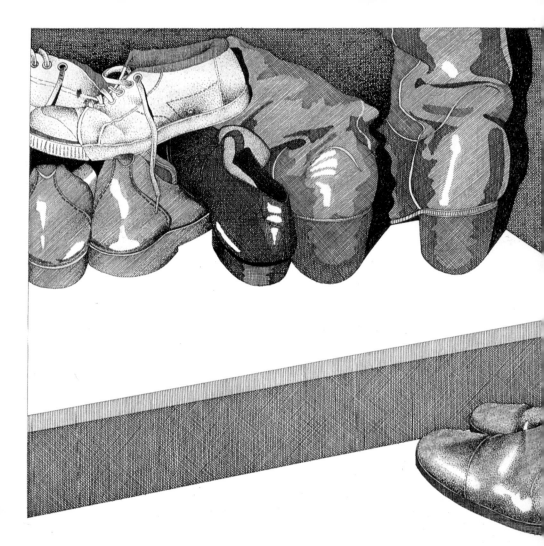

THE DIFFERENCE BETWEEN A SHOE AND A DUCK

You will notice a shoe has a leather cross-section
and ducks leave unbearable dung.
(To distinguish the two by internal inspection
is hard, for they both have a tongue).

DUCK

In Memory of a Much Travelled Ornithologist who Lost her Powers of Reason:

"Though I've studied birds for years,
(I've noticed very few have ears)
most of all, their daily feeding
takes up almost all my reading:
did you know in dead tree hollows
hide the crows that swallow swallows.....

......hawks eat cheese from far-off cultures,
vultures just eat other vultures;
(crimes like these are found in others:
plovers eat their husbands' mothers)......

(3)

......Though the spotted redshank nibbles
fairy cakes, it seldom dribbles
when it's drinking cups of mustard.
(Little bustards live on custard).
Though this list could be extended;
this is where I'll stop."

                              She ended.

29

BURIED TREASURE AND THE WIMP

Withered sailors at the seaside,
   bent, with trousers rolled:
sieving gravel, lifting boulders,
   searching sand for gold.
Never one for probing rockpools
   I was not so bold;
While the birds were catching oysters
   I just caught a cold.

swan up, duck down, fish out, larks about

32

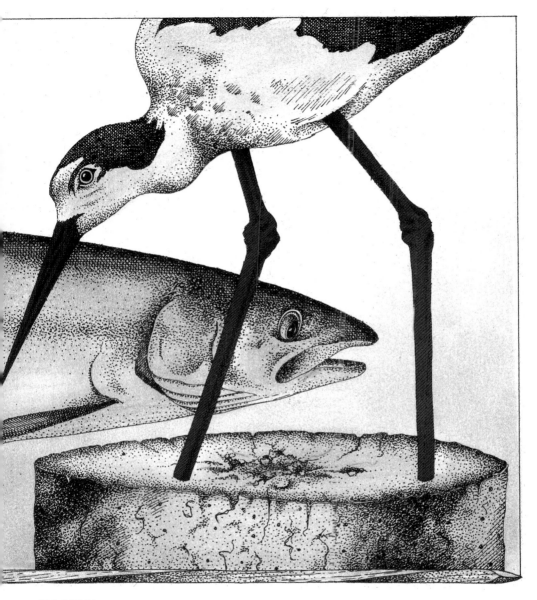

menu:
snails on skewers grilled with garlic;
hot welsh rarebit (cheese of Harlech);
cold scotch salmon (fish with kilt on);
goose on brie and stilt on stilton.

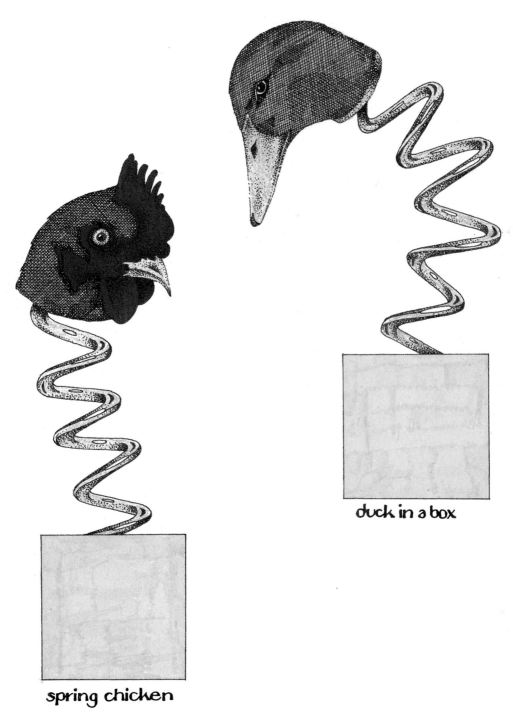

spring chicken

duck in a box

EIDER WAY UP

EIDER WAY UP

grandfather was an inventor,
(though his efforts were modest, you'll see):
while others were splitting the atom
he tried to improve on our tea.

was the thing I saw a burning K ?
that's what I would really like to know.
maybe I had seen a blazing A
or could it just have been a flaming O ?

"Where is my dinner?
I'm feeling much thinner"
(Uncle Sebastian was shouting from bed).
"Too late my darling
I've swallowed a starling"
(Uncle Sebastian was turning quite red).
"Here comes the train, dear;
The guard is a reindeer"
(Uncle Sebastian had gone off his head).

FRANCE'S DRAKE

WATER OFF A DUCK'S BACK

BATTERY HEN

The birds below have almost reached extinction:
not killed by fire or storm or tremor,
but wrangling politicians of distinction
impaled them on the horns of a dilemma.

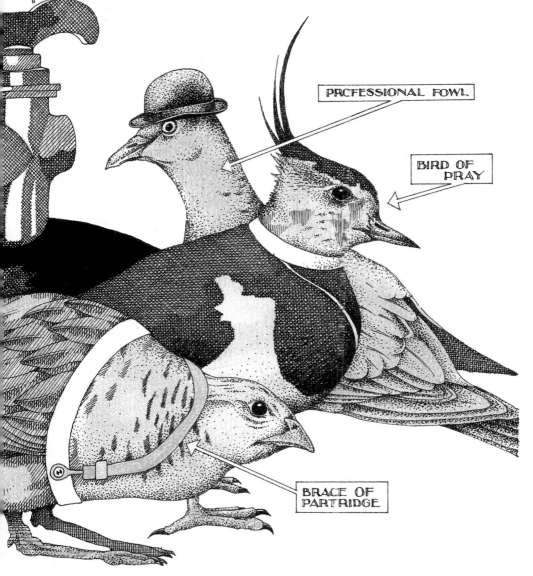

PROFESSIONAL FOWL

BIRD OF PRAY

BRACE OF PARTRIDGE

IN PRAISE OF FISHY DINNERS

From the depth of souls and oceans
can it be denied:
any bird that lives on herring
must have brains inside.

HOW TO PUT A SHIP IN A BOTTLE...

1

First of all you fetch some paper
wood and bits of string:
then construct the perfect schooner,
strength must be the thing.

2

Now a bottle: this is crucial.
Don't pick one too thin.
If you're making something special
choose one made for gin.

3

But this bottle must be empty
(letting in the boat).
Place the contents in a tumbler
then transfer to throat.

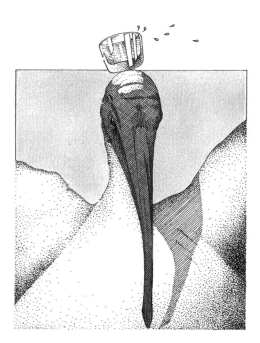

4

Now you'll sing a rousing chorus
as you dance a jig;
(though the ship's not in the bottle
you won't give a fig).

"wendy and I"
by simon drew
dartmouth devon

Christmas last year at dinner
they told us we could pick
all of the food we wanted:
our minds were made up quick.
Wendy and I chose ice cream
and lollies on a stick:
Wendy and I chose jellies
with custard one inch thick:
Wendy and I chose chocolate
Wendy and I were sick.

once bittern twice shy

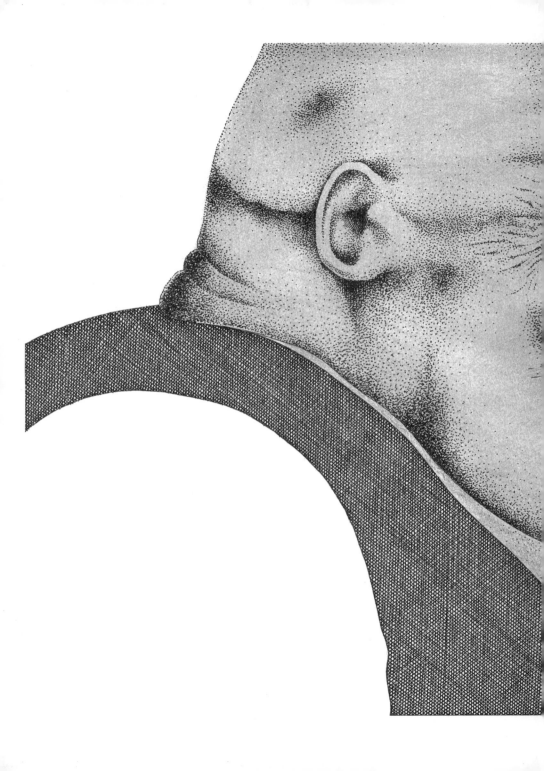

This book belongs to

_____

This edition published by Parragon in 2012
Parragon
Queen Street House
4 Queen Street
Bath BA1 1HE, UK
www.parragon.com

Copyright © Parragon Books Ltd 2004

Written by Jillian Harker   Illustrated by Kristina Stephenson

All rights reserved. No part of this publication may be reproduced, stored in a
retrieval system or transmitted, in any form or by any means, electronic, mechanical,
photocopying, recording or otherwise, without the prior permission of the
copyright holder.

ISBN 978-1-4454-9561-3

Printed in China

I Love You,
Mommy

PaRRaGon

Bath · New York · Singapore · Hong Kong · Cologne · Delhi
Melbourne · Amsterdam · Johannesburg · Shenzhen

"Watch me, Mommy," called Little Bear.
"I'm going fishing."
"Just a minute," replied Mommy Bear.
"There's something you might want to know."

But Little Bear was already
running down to the river.

Mommy Bear ran, too.

She saw Little Bear
jump onto a rock.

She saw Little
Bear reach out
his paw to
catch a fish.

Then Little Bear began to teeter and totter.

"This doesn't feel so good!" thought Little Bear.

"Good try!" smiled Mommy Bear. "But watch me now, Little Bear."
Little Bear watched Mommy Bear paddle around and around.
"Your turn now, Little Bear," she said.

Little Bear did exactly what Mommy Bear did.
"This feels good!" thought Little Bear.
"I love Mommy."

"Watch me, Mommy," called Little Bear.
"I'm going to pick that fruit."
"Just a minute," replied Mommy Bear. "There's something you might want to know."

But Little Bear was
already climbing the tree.

Mommy Bear saw
Little Bear run
along a branch.

She saw Little Bear
reach out his paw to
pick some juicy fruit.

Then Little Bear began to wiggle and wobble.

CRASH!

"This doesn't feel like fun!" thought Little Bear.

"Not bad!" said Mommy Bear. "But watch me now, Little Bear."

Little Bear watched how Mommy Bear balanced as she climbed. "Your turn now, Little Bear," she said.

Little Bear did what Mommy Bear did.
"This tastes good!" thought Little Bear.
"I love Mommy."

"Look, Mommy," smiled Little Bear. "All the other cubs are playing. I'm going to play, too." "Wait a minute, please," said Mommy Bear. "There's something you might want to know."

Little Bear turned. "Tell me, please," he said.
"Be gentle when you play," said Mommy Bear.
"Like this." Mommy Bear reached out her paws.
She wrapped her arms around Little Bear. She
rolled Little Bear over and over on the ground.

"I love Mommy," thought Little Bear. Then he ran away to play. He did just what Mommy Bear had done.

And it felt like

fun!

Little Bear was very tired when he got home,
but there was something he wanted to say.
"I wanted to tell you," said Little Bear.
"Yes?" said Mommy Bear.

"I love you, M ..."
But Little Bear didn't finish.

Mommy Bear kissed Little Bear's sleepy head.

"I love you, too." she said.